Published and sold by E. Sachse & Co. Baltimore Md.

CITY OF ANNAPOLIS,

STATE OF MARYLAND.

Annapolis on the *Chesapeake*

Herb and Elaine —
We hope to see
you in Annapolis in
the near future!
Gerry,
Sandy,
nikki
and ross
3/98

For three hundred years Annapolis has been a sylvan Venice where land and water intermingle; hence, no view of it is more characteristic than what mariners see when entering Spa Creek bound for the "Dock." The inset shows the State House dome as it appeared to an artist nearly two centuries ago.

Annapolis
on the
Chesapeake

TEXT BY

Arthur Pierce Middleton

PHOTOGRAPHY BY

N. Jane Iseley

Historic Annapolis, Incorporated
Annapolis, Maryland
and
Legacy Publications, *A Subsidiary of*
Pace Communications
Greensboro, North Carolina

ACKNOWLEDGEMENTS

Among the many people who have helped, the authors wish to acknowledge in particular the following team members:

St. Clair Wright, Pringle Symonds, Patricia Kohlhepp, Jean Lee Eareckson, Jane Anderson, Julie Fife, Edward C. Papenfuse, Phebe Jacobsen, Mame Warren, Steven C. Newsome, Mrs. Coleman Dupont, Barbara A. Brand, Frederica Struse, Orlando Ridout IV, Richard Stinely, Lil Baldwin, Andy and Boots Michalak, Janice B. Strain, Debra J. Bost, and Steve Cernak.

Library of Congress
Catalog Card Number: 88-82125

ISBN 0-933101-13-9 (Hardback Edition)
ISBN 0-933101-14-7 (Softback Edition)

Designed by Richard Stinely
Edited by Debra J. Bost

*Printed in Hong Kong
by Everbest Printing Company
through Four Colour Imports Ltd.,
Louisville, Kentucky.*

With admiration and gratitude
this book is dedicated to

St. Clair Wright

The quintessential visionary who
more than anyone else saved
historic Annapolis for the future.

Annapolis from the Air. Governor Nicholson's town plan of 1695 is still discernible from the air. The State House and St. Anne's Church are centered on two circles from which streets radiate like the spokes of a wheel.

ANNAPOLIS emerged in the eighteenth century as the foremost seaport of Maryland. Conveniently situated on a deepwater tributary of the broad Severn River, in sight of Chesapeake Bay, the city became the crossroads of planters, lawyers, and merchants of the province, and the center of fashion and entertainment. Apart from periodic visits to Annapolis, prosperous plantation society enjoyed few opportunities to engage in large-scale social activities. As a result, Annapolis became the hub of Maryland's import trade in luxury goods from abroad.

After the Revolution, when ships became too large for the depth of the Annapolis harbor, the rising city of Baltimore overtook it as the great seaport of Maryland, and for a century and a half the maritime economy of Annapolis was largely confined to Chesapeake Bay transport and fisheries. But history often has a strange way of unfolding in cycles, and the second half of the twentieth century has witnessed just such a development. While the great tankers and cargo vessels still head for Baltimore, the shallower creeks of Annapolis have become filled with yachts and marinas supplied by boatbuilders, sailmakers, shipchandlers, and marine insurance agents.

When the early settlers sailed between Cape Henry and Cape Charles, they found awaiting them what was to be the determining factor in the development of Virginia and Maryland for centuries to come: they found Chesapeake Bay. Landlocked except for a dozen miles between the capes, this noble body of water extended nearly two hundred miles north and south, and had nearly fifty naviga-ble tributaries thrusting long tidal reaches inland, some of them for as much as one hundred miles. These in turn had more than one hundred navigable branches and creeks of various length, depth, and configuration. Together they interlaced thousands of square miles of woodlands and arable soil, thus providing the settlers with access to the interior by means of a natural system of waterways not found anywhere else. As a result, the two Chesapeake colonies became a land of plantations strung along the banks of rivers and creeks capable of receiving ships from abroad. For more than a century cities and towns were economically unnecessary. Jamestown, the capital of Virginia from 1607 to 1699, and St. Mary's, the capital of Maryland from 1634 to 1694, were no more than small villages. Both faded away as soon as the government of Maryland moved to Annapolis in 1695, and that of Virginia to Williamsburg in 1699.

Tobacco, the staple of Virginia and Maryland, was the chief influence in their colonial economy and style of life. Tobacco resulted in the plantation system; the importation of cheap labor, such as indentured servants, slaves, and convicts; and the dispersion of the population. But it was the Chesapeake and its tributaries that enabled tobacco to be grown in enormous quantities. Tobacco will grow in many places. What made Virginia and Maryland unique was not better soil but the system of waterways which, in the days before railroads and hard-surfaced highways, made all the difference. Tobacco is a bulky commodity; its delicate leaf sustained damage and lost value if the half-ton hogsheads were rolled very far or carted as much as twenty miles over rough roads. This meant that it could only be grown in quantity near water carriage, and Chesapeake Bay provided just that. Thanks to this natural resource, Virginia and Maryland produced tobacco on a grand scale. Nearly one hundred thousand hogsheads containing one hundred million pounds of tobacco were exported in 1775 alone.

For the first century or so the ever-increasing waves of incoming settlers from the Mother Country claimed land conveniently located along navigable rivers and creeks. They could import European goods and export tobacco in seagoing vessels anchored within a stone's throw of their plantation landing. As long as the population was confined to the coastal plain there was no economic reason for the growth of towns. Indeed, the entire Chesapeake tidewater was one gigantic seaport!

After about 1700, however, when the tidewater lands were largely taken up, the never-ending stream of immigrants faced a choice: They could become tenant farmers or go up into the Piedmont on the Western Shore rivers where land was still available. When the latter happened, they no longer enjoyed the convenience of seagoing vessels anchoring at their plantation wharves. Ships from overseas were obliged to unload below the falls or rapids that marked the intersection of the Piedmont plateau and the low-lying coastal plain. The goods had to be stored in warehouses until they could be carted inland to planters, whose tobacco and grain had to be poled downstream in flatboats to the fall line for export in seagoing vessels. As a result, the eighteenth century witnessed the rise of a series of important towns that ultimately became the cities of today: Baltimore on the Patapsco, Washington on the Potomac, and Richmond on the James.

The profusion of navigable waterways and the abundance of timber stimulated the growth of shipbuilding. In colonial days, the industry was widely distributed around the Bay rather than concentrated as it later became. Colonial Annapolis enjoyed a share in it, and developed such ancillary trades as sailmakers, ropewalks, blockmakers, ironmasters, and shipchandlers, making it Maryland's most important marine supply center by the middle of the eighteenth century.

But Annapolis had not always been a bustling town, throbbing with life. In 1695, it was an unimpressive village of wooden houses with fewer than 250 inhabitants. Puritan nonconformists from Virginia seeking freedom of worship had settled at the mouth of the Severn River in 1649. There were settlers on the site of Annapolis early in the 1650's, and a shipyard was in operation soon afterwards. But economic conditions did not favor the growth of Arundelton, as it was called, until it became the capital of Maryland in 1695. By that time the lands around the upper Chesapeake had been settled and the original capital, St. Mary's, near the mouth of the Potomac River, proved to be inconveniently located for most Marylanders. In 1694, the energetic royal governor, Francis Nicholson, induced the General Assembly to move the seat of government to the more centrally located Arundelton. It was renamed Annapolis in 1695 in honor of the the next in line of royal succession after the reigning King William III, Princess Anne, who was destined to become Queen Anne in 1702.

DURING the years following 1695, Annapolis was laid out according to a sophisticated and typically baroque plan devised by Governor Nicholson. As the town occupies a peninsula and is distinguished by two hills, he created a circle on the crest of each hill and made the streets radiate from both State and Church circles like spokes of a wheel. To this was added a grid of streets intersecting one another at right angles. A simplified version of contemporary designs by city planners in Paris and London, the result was virtually unique in America until L'Enfant's plan for the City of Washington a century later. Both were influenced by the layout of King Louis XIV's palace of Versailles. Although the governor's baroque plan created odd-shaped lots like pieces of pie, which have caused inconvenience to the inhabitants ever since, visitors are compensated by charming irreg-

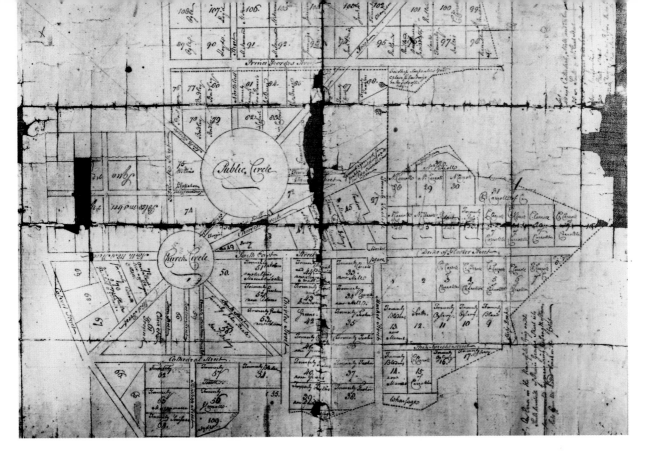

In 1718 John Stoddert made a "Ground Plot of the City of Annapolis" showing State and Church circles and the streets that radiate from them. The town dock is also conspicuous because of its commercial importance.

ularities and picturesque views of the town's two principal buildings, the State House and St. Anne's Church, around which the life and traffic of Annapolis have flowed for nearly three centuries.

Even with the erection of the state house and church and with the governor in residence, the town grew slowly. The great planters preferred to live along the navigable rivers instead of in Annapolis. Gradually, however, the community at the mouth of the Severn took hold and began to grow. Annapolis was granted a city charter in 1708. The weekly *Maryland Gazette* began publication in 1727, faltered, and began its continuous existence in 1745. As the population of Maryland grew, so did the number of proprietary officials, most of whom found it convenient to live in Annapolis or at least to maintain a house here. King William's School, chartered in 1696, was in operation by 1700. The first state house, built in 1695–1697 and destroyed by fire in 1704, was immediately rebuilt on its original foundations. The first St. Anne's Church, begun in the 1690's and completed about 1704, was the only church in

Annapolis until the Revolution. There was an immediate and continuing need for taverns to accommodate members of the General Assembly, travelers, lawyers and litigants in cases before the provincial courts. One of the early taverns was the Kentish Inn. Others bore the names of their owners or had characteristically eighteenth-century names like the Lord Baltimore Arms, the Sign of the Ship, the Sign of the Duke of Cumberland, and the Crown and Dial. Yet another in 1773 rejoiced in the name of the Sign of the Indian King. The number of inns and taverns indicates that the town supported a relatively large transient population during the "Publick Times" when the assembly and courts were in session.

Among the earliest tradesmen in Annapolis were shipwrights, tanners, and shoemakers. Because of the abundance of timber in America and its shortage in Great Britain, ships were built more cheaply than in the Mother Country, and Chesapeake Bay and its tributaries made it necessary for Marylanders to have boats for local transportation as well as for trade to Great Britain and

9

Shiplap House, *18 Pinkney Street.* Built about 1713, this was a part of the earliest business area in Annapolis. Edward Smith, a sawyer, kept a tavern here in 1718. In the years 1738–1748, a shipbuilder, Ashbury Sutton, lived here. About the time of the Revolution, it was occupied by John Humphrey who kept the "Harp & Crown" tavern here. From 1817 to 1877 it was owned by a Scottish cabinetmaker, John Slicer, and his family, followed by the noted Maryland artist, Frank B. Mayer, whose patriotic canvas, "The Burning of the *Peggy Stewart*," hangs in the State House. Down Pinkney Street on the right is the Tobacco Prize House, where the role of tobacco in colonial Maryland is interpreted to visitors.

A view of the brick end of the weather-boarded Shiplap House. The first floor has been fitted out to depict a colonial tavern and to display selected artifacts excavated by the Urban Archaelogy Program cosponsored by the University of Maryland and Historic Annapolis.

the West Indies. The abundance of cattle created a useful raw material and provided opportunities for tanners and shoemakers. As shipping increased, so did the trades that supplied its needs: sailmakers, ropemakers, ironworkers, and shipchandlers. In 1745, Thomas Fleming did a thriving business "at the Sign of the top-sail Sheet Block" near the Annapolis market house selling "all Sorts of Blocks for Shipping" and making pumps for vessels. A few years later Nicholas Maccubbin and Lancelot Jacques were his competitors. As early as 1736, an Irish sailmaker, John Conner, was plying his trade in Annapolis, and by 1753 he had a competitor, William Bicknell. Before the middle of the eighteenth century there were several covered ropewalks in Annapolis, one of them 360 feet long. Several ironworks appeared in the upper part of the Bay early in the century. One of them, the Baltimore Iron Works, began in 1731 as a joint venture of five gentlemen, four of them Annapolis residents. Another was the Patuxent Iron Works in nearby Prince George's County. These ironworks made large profits for the investors and soon produced enough iron both to meet local needs and to export in quantity to Great Britain. By 1750, Maryland iron amounted to half the total exported from all the American colonies, and to one-seventh of England's production of iron.

Among the important shipbuilders in colonial Annapolis was Ashbury Sutton, who occupied the Shiplap House at 18 Pinkney Street in the 1730's, owned a ropewalk in Annapolis, and operated a sailing ferry to the Eastern Shore. Another was Patrick Creagh, whose house can still be seen at 160 Prince George Street. Creagh built the Old Treasury Building on State Circle about 1735, and what is now McDowell Hall of St. John's College in 1742. He also built a small fleet of merchant vessels. Between 1734 and 1749, he owned fourteen vessels totaling 790 tons. A competitor, Levin Gale, owned nine vessels of 432 tons at about the same time. Another Annapolitan, William Roberts, owned a 400-ton ship in 1746, as well as one of 150 tons. These vessels were probably built in Annapolis shipyards, and perhaps some of them on the ship carpenter's lot laid out in the original town plan on the northern side of the town dock.

Thanks to the expanding population, carpenters and bricklayers were needed from the start, and as time went by and wealth accumulated, a demand arose for more skilled craftsmen such as masons, woodcarvers, and plasterers. Finally, of course, there arose a need for professional architects. Until well along in the eighteenth century, however, the prevailing custom was to erect utilitarian buildings in the vernacular fashion. If something more elaborate was desired, a gentleman could always design his own home with the help, perhaps, of books from Great Britain with engravings of contemporary houses, doorways, and mantelpieces. Hence there was little need for professional architects until late in the colonial period.

IN 1742, Governor Thomas Bladen secured an appropriation of £4000 to build a governor's mansion in Annapolis, now McDowell Hall of St. John's College. Not feeling up to designing so grand a building, he sent to Great Britain for a plan which was brought from Glasgow by Simon Duff. Presumably Duff drew the plan, but the actual construction was undertaken by Patrick Creagh, whom we have already met in his capacity of shipbuilder. When the twenty-three-year old William Paca began his house and garden in 1763, he appears to have designed it himself, relying no doubt upon English books for ideas. The same was probably true of most of the other great houses built during the Golden Age of Annapolis. One notable exception is the Hammond-Harwood House, built in 1774. It was designed by a professional architect, William Buckland (1740–1774), and is perhaps the most sophisticated example of Palladian architecture in the town, if not in America.

Other architects in late eighteenth-century Annapolis include Joseph Horatio Anderson (d. 1774) who designed the present State House in 1772 and also the second St. Anne's Church shortly afterwards, and Joseph Clark (d. 1798) who was born in England, apprenticed to a London joiner in

St. Anne's Church

Church Circle. The interior of St. Anne's Church is in Romanesque Revival style. The stone altar and font were carved by Maryland's foremost sculptor, William Henry Rinehart (1825–1874). The bishop's chair, pulpit, and walnut pews date from 1859. The brass eagle lectern is a memorial to Captain James Waddell (1824–1886) who, as master of the Confederate raider *Shenandoah,* was said to have taken or sunk more American vessels than anyone else in history. The walnut reredos depicting the risen Christ offering the Book of Life to the world was done in 1920 by the Oberammergau woodcarver, William Kirchmayer.

A prospect of the town as seen from the new front of the State House, completed about 1905.

1742, and lived in Annapolis 1774–1794. He designed the present wooden dome on the State House and oversaw its construction in the years 1785–1788.

Being the provincial capital and the residence of the governor, Annapolis became the regular meeting place of the leading families of Maryland. Many people came not only for the sessions of the General Assembly and courts but also for the social festivities that accompanied them: banquets, balls, card parties, horse races, and the theatre. In consequence, shopkeepers who dealt in luxury items found Annapolis a strategic location for their shops. Silversmiths, goldsmiths, and watchmakers appeared here early in the eighteenth century. At first they found little opportunity to make anything original other than simple items. It was more profitable to import English luxury goods to sell, engrave crests on silver for the local gentry, and repair broken teapot spouts and handles. Tobacco planters produced a crop that was in demand in Great Britain. Unlike the wealthy inhabitants of the Northern colonies, they had ready access to sterling credits and could indulge their nostalgia for the Mother Country by buying imported furnishings in the latest London fashion. This innate desire to "buy British" tended to confine local craftsmen to a subsidiary role. After the Stamp Act in 1765 and the nonimportation agreements it provoked, the situation changed abruptly. It became not only acceptable but even patriotic to patronize "country" craftsmen and to resist the ingrained temptation to buy British goods.

Among the earliest silversmiths in Annapolis were two Huguenots whose parents had fled to England after the Revocation of the Edict of Nantes, thereby depriving them of freedom of worship in France. They learned their trade in England and migrated to America as adults. Cesar Ghiselin (c. 1670–1734) worked in Philadelphia from 1701 to 1716, in Annapolis from 1716 to 1728, and then returned to Philadelphia. Samuel Soumaien (c. 1718–1765) practiced as a silversmith in Annapolis from 1740 to 1754, and like so many other skilled craftsmen moved to Philadelphia in search of better patronage. While here, he lived on the upper end

Continued on page 17

Three successive churches on this site have served St. Anne's Parish since its creation in 1692 by the General Assembly as one of thirty parishes of the Church of England in the province. King William III sent a set of communion silver, made in 1696, to his Chapel Royal in Maryland, and it is still in use.

19 Maryland Avenue. Noted for its fine brickwork, handsome doorway, and perfect Georgian proportions, this gem of a late colonial mansion was designed by the architect William Buckland in 1774 for a wealthy planter and lawyer, Mathias Hammond, who was active in the anti-proprietary or "Country party." Later owners included Ninian Pinkney, brother of the statesman William Pinkney, and Jeremiah Townley Chase, a judge, mayor of Annapolis, and cousin of Samuel Chase the "Signer." Jeremiah's granddaughter married William Harwood, the great-grandson of the architect, and their daughter, Hester Anne Harwood, lived in the house until her death in 1924.

William Buckland (1734-1774) by Charles Willson Peale. Born in England and apprenticed to a London joiner, Buckland was brought to Virginia in 1755 by George Mason to finish Gunston Hall, his fine home on the Potomac. He later worked for other Virginia planters, including Colonel John Tayloe of Mt. Airy whose daughter had married Edward Lloyd IV. As a result of that connection, Lloyd brought Buckland to Annapolis in 1771 to work on the Chase-Lloyd House. It was here that the gifted young man found the opportunity to create his masterpiece, the Hammond-Harwood House.

Yale University Art Gallery
Mabel Brady Garvan Collection

Rising seventeen feet above the level of the sidewalk, this superb doorway, with its carved roses, is considered to be among the most beautiful of American survivals from colonial days. The design is believed to be original with William Buckland and not copied from architectural books of the period.

Hammond-Harwood House

The ballroom has a jib door that opens to brick steps leading to the garden. The mansion is maintained by the Hammond-Harwood House Association, formed half a century ago, has a magnificent collection of period furniture, and is open to the public.

Detail of carving on the shutter.

The portrait of the six-year-old Ann Procter holding her favorite wooden doll was painted by Charles Willson Peale in January 1789. Both the portrait and the actual doll were preserved by Ann's descendants and given to the Association.

Hammond-Harwood House

The drawing room on the second floor (a rarity in pre-Revolutionary Annapolis, although common in Philadelphia) has rich carving on the mantel that echoes the rose and ribbon motif on the front door. Apparently it was original with Buckland as nothing like it has been found in any of the British books of design that were available to him.

The Library Chamber is furnished with a chest of drawers by John Shaw with a dated label, 1795, and a Chippendale chair attributed to him because of its similarity to the chairs he made for the Senate Chamber.

The garden front differs from the street front by being adorned with massive brick pilasters and a full entablature giving a suggestion, when seen from a slight distance, of a temple portico.

of the Duke of Gloucester Street until 1749 when he moved to Main Street, then called Church Street. Considering the difficulties that early silversmiths encountered in Annapolis, it is scarcely surprising that in addition to silver, he sold hops, rum, and Madeira, and served as an auctioneer.

THERE were several other silversmiths in Annapolis who combined their craft with tavern-keeping. John Inch (1720–1763) was one of them. He was working in Annapolis by about 1741, and in 1743 made a silver bowl to serve as a trophy for the first recorded formal horse race in Maryland. The bowl is now considered to be the oldest major surviving piece of Maryland silver. Originally on Duke of Gloucester Street, Inch moved in 1749 to the dock area where he opened a tavern and also dealt in gold, silver, clocks, and watches. To be on the safe side, he also sold sugar, hired out boats, offered to do house painting, and sold indentured servants. William Faris, Sr. (1728–1804), a native Londoner who settled here in 1757, was a watchmaker, silversmith, cabinetmaker, portrait painter, dentist, and tavern-keeper as well, but today he is remembered chiefly for his diary which covers many years and enshrines much of the town's uninhibited gossip of his day. Yet another silversmith, John Chalmers (c. 1750–c. 1819), who worked in Annapolis from 1765 to about 1791, is best known for the silver coins—a shilling, a sixpence, and a threepence—that he issued in 1783, apparently without formal authority from the state government.

The demand for furniture in colonial Maryland, especially among the well-to-do planters, was largely supplied by British-made imports. This strong preference discouraged the growth of local cabinetmakers in the tobacco colonies. Only after 1765 was there a sudden reversal, and it became patriotic and fashionable for the first time to buy American-made furnishings. The rise of skilled and prosperous cabinetmakers did not take place in the Southern colonies until the last third of the

eighteenth century. With few exceptions, furniture made below the Mason-Dixon Line—and certainly in Annapolis—before that time was generally plain and utilitarian in character rather than decorated in high style. For that reason, there arose no distinctive local type of furniture in Annapolis as was the case in Boston, New York, and Philadelphia. Distinctive Maryland furniture belongs largely to the post-Revolutionary period. Of the several late eighteenth-century Annapolis cabinetmakers, the best known and most prolific was John Shaw (1745–1829), a Scotsman who came to Annapolis from Glasgow in 1763 at the age of eighteen and who worked here for fifty years. His patrons included members of such prominent Annapolis families as the Lloyds, Ridouts, Carrolls, Pacas, Ogles, Chases, Pinkneys, and Randalls. Nearly fifty documented Shaw pieces still exist as well as others that are attributed to him. He is said to have perpetuated the vogue in Annapolis for transitional Chippendale-Federal furniture based on English fashions. Because of the relative simplicity of his furniture, he was able to produce it in quantity and to expand his business at a time when Baltimore was eclipsing Annapolis as the social and economic metropolis of Maryland. Shaw was the last cabinetmaker in Annapolis to enjoy a flourishing trade. In addition, he is remembered for supervising the construction and maintenance of the present State House and other public buildings, and for making and repairing furniture for the State. He also served in the Maryland militia. Locally, he was a vestryman of St. Anne's Parish, an alderman of the City of Annapolis, and the official keeper of the town's fire engine.

The increasing wealth of merchants, lawyers, and the landed gentry, and the fact that they built larger houses as the eighteenth century progressed and had wallspace for pictures, soon created a market for "limners" or portrait painters. A German artist, Justus Engelhardt Kuhn, appeared in Annapolis in 1708, applied for naturalization, and found the prosperous inhabitants of the town and province willing to patronize him. He remained here and practiced his profession until his death in 1717. Soon afterwards a Swedish portrait painter,

Continued on page 21

The State House

Begun in 1772 and in use after 1779, this is the oldest state capitol still in use. From November 26, 1783 until August 13, 1784, it housed the Continental Congress, giving Annapolis the distinction of having been the capital of the United States for nearly nine months.

Designed and built by the architect Joseph Clark, this splendid wooden dome replaced an earlier, shallower one in 1785–1788, and has been a landmark for residents, visitors, and yachtsmen ever since.

The increased size of the General Assembly resulted in the addition of a western extension, containing larger chambers for its two houses. The present House of Delegates Chamber, completed in 1905, is in a modified Italian-Renaissance style with marble columns, vaulted arcades, and a Tiffany skylight of stained glass.

The doors of the new front of the State House proudly display the coat-of-arms of Maryland, derived from the armorial bearings granted by James I to Sir George Calvert, who was later elevated to the peerage as Lord Baltimore. His son, Cecil, received the Charter for Maryland from Charles I in 1632.

The State House

Here in the Old Senate Chamber on December 23, 1783, General George Washington resigned his commission as commander-in-chief of the Continental Army, and on January 14, 1784, Congress ratified the Treaty of Paris which ended the Revolutionary War and obtained formal British recognition of American Independence.

The hall of the State House with its great columns and high ceiling must have been the most impressive room in Maryland when it was built in the 1770's. The fine Adam style plasterwork in the interior of the dome was completed in 1793 and was the work of Thomas Dance, who fell to his death from the scaffolding just as he finished his masterpiece.

Gustavus Hesselius (1682–1755) settled in Prince George's County and traveled in both Maryland and Virginia in quest of commissions. He did portraits of several prominent Annapolitans, including Thomas Bordley (1682–1726), attorney general of Maryland and builder of the Bordley-Randall House, and Mary Darnall Carroll (1679–1742), whose son built the Carroll House behind the present St. Mary's Church, and whose grandson, Charles Carroll of Carrollton, was a signer of the Declaration of Independence. Although Gustavus Hesselius moved to Philadelphia about 1730, he continued to make periodic visits to Maryland for commissions. His son, John Hesselius (d. 1778), followed in his father's footsteps and became an even better portrait painter. He settled in Anne Arundel County and through marriage to a widow in 1763 acquired a plantation near Annapolis, Primrose Hill. In the following fifteen years he painted likenesses of many Marylanders and also gave lessons in painting to a young saddler in Annapolis, Charles Willson Peale.

An English portrait painter, John Wollaston, came to Maryland in 1752 after sojourning in New York and Philadelphia, and became the local exemplar of the rococo style, which was in vogue in Europe and was well suited to the tastes of the tobacco aristocracy. Wollaston left Maryland for greener pastures in Virginia sometime before 1755. Despite his short stay, he had no difficulty in obtaining commissions and painted no fewer than sixty portraits for the Bordley, Calvert, Carroll, and Dulany families of Annapolis and their social peers throughout Maryland.

Best known of all was Charles Willson Peale (1741–1827) who was born in Queen Anne's County on the Eastern Shore and came to Annapolis as a young man to be apprenticed to a saddler. While here, he began to paint signs for which there was a growing demand. Showing talent, he studied under John Hesselius and in 1767 was sent to London by a group of Maryland gentlemen, including William Paca, to study under the great master, Benjamin West. To show his appreciation, Peale painted a full-length portrait of the English statesman, William Pitt, gave it to the citizens of Maryland,

Government Buildings. From the new front of the State House one can see state office buildings erected in recent decades in a Georgian style to blend with the distinctive architectural decor of Annapolis.

Old Treasury Building. This substantially built cruciform structure was erected about 1736 to house the commissioners appointed under an act of 1733 to issue paper money for the Province of Maryland. At a later date it housed the state treasurer, which accounts for its traditional name. Restored in 1949, the Old Treasury building now serves as the tour office of Historic Annapolis.

Governor's Mansion. Built shortly
after the Civil War, this mansion has
housed every governor of Maryland
since 1870. Originally Victorian in
appearance, complete with mansard roof
and spacious porches, it was remodeled
in 1935 and given a facade more in
keeping with its Georgian neighbors.

Anne Arundel County Courthouse,
Church Circle. This picturesque
building, which echoes some of the
lines of the State House dome, is the
end product of several additions. It was
built in 1824, remodeled in 1892, and
further enlarged in 1952.

and it can still be seen in the Annapolis State House. After his return in 1769, Peale's reputation spread to neighboring colonies, and in 1776 he moved to Philadelphia, then the largest city in English America, where his ability and dedication to the American cause won him acclaim and prosperity. He painted no fewer than sixty portraits of George Washington, seven of them from life, and they were considered by his contemporaries to be faithful likenesses. Among Peale's portraits of Annapolitans are those of Edward Lloyd and family painted in 1771, William Paca in 1772, Mrs. Samuel Chase and daughters in 1772–1775, William Buckland in 1774, and Sarah and Mary Callahan in 1791. Peale's brother James was also an artist and is remembered chiefly for his miniatures. And Charles Willson Peale not only named several of his children after famous artists— Raphael, Rembrandt, and Titian—but also imbued them with the love of painting and launched them on artistic careers. On one occasion, when Washington sat for portraits by both Charles Willson Peale and one of his sons, the otherwise staid Virginia gentleman was reported to have declared that he was "well Pealed."

The most popular entertainment in colonial Maryland was gaming in all of its forms, but especially at cards and in connection with horse racing. It is no wonder that they made their appearance at an early date in Annapolis, where the most elegant card parties in Maryland and the most spectacular races were held. By the middle of the eighteenth century English fanciers of horseflesh had imported three thoroughbreds from the Middle East to improve their native stock, and it was not long before their Maryland counterparts brought over foals of these strains. Governor Samuel Ogle, his successor, Governor Horatio Sharpe, and Ogle's brother-in-law, Colonel Benjamin Tasker, were racing buffs and among the first in America to import Arabian horses. As early as 1750, Tasker brought "Selima," a mare descended from the famous "Godolphin Arabian," to his Maryland stables and bred her to Governor Sharpe's "Othello," also descended from the "Godolphin Arabian." The resulting offspring, "Selim," became the most suc-

Continued on page 26

City Hall, *Duke of Gloucester and Market streets.*
Here was erected in 1766–1769 a brick building that housed the Revenue Office of Lord Baltimore, and that also served as a ballroom where many gala assemblies were held—some of them attended by George Washington. Gutted by fire while occupied by the Federal forces during the Civil War, it was rebuilt incorporating the colonial walls, enlarged, and adorned with a Victorian facade in 1867. Since 1870 it has served as the city hall of Annapolis.

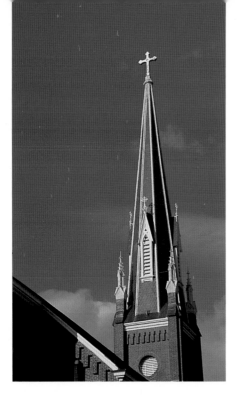

The steeple of St. Mary's Church, like that of St. Anne's, presents a pleasing appearance when seen from various parts of the city, and especially when gilded by the setting sun.

St. Mary's Church, *Duke of Gloucester Street.* Although "Papists" in eighteenth-century Maryland were forbidden to build churches prior to the Revolution, they were allowed to hold services in private homes. The Carrolls' chapel on the upper floor of their house on Spa Creek was the principal Roman Catholic place of worship in colonial Annapolis. Enjoying religious freedom after the Revolution, they built a small church on the site of the present parish school in 1825. It was replaced in 1858-1860 by the present St. Mary's Church, a Gothic Revival structure with a pleasing interior.

Carroll House. Charles Carroll of Annapolis (1702–1782), a wealthy landowner, built a brick house about 1727 which was later enlarged several times. His son, Charles Carroll of Carrollton (1737–1832), a signer of the Declaration of Independence, is thought to have been born here, and it was his Annapolis home until 1800. Unlike their distant cousins, Dr. Charles Carroll and his son, Charles Carroll the Barrister, who were Episcopalians, these Carrolls were among the leading Roman Catholics in Maryland. Although excluded by their religion from active participation in politics until the Revolution, they were active in the economic and social life of colonial Maryland and handsomely entertained the colonial "big wigs" at their hospitable home. The property was given to the Redemptorists in 1852 by Carroll descendants and the mansion houses the Second Novitiate of the Order. Just below the spire of St. Mary's and distinguished by massive chimneys is the Carroll House.

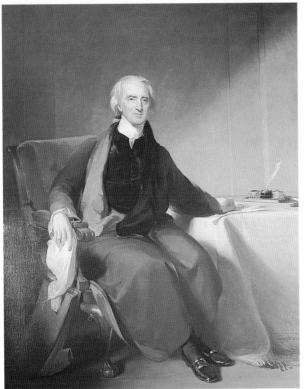

Charles Carroll of Carrollton (1737–1832) by Sully. The only son of his father, he was sent abroad for his education at Jesuit college in Flanders, at Paris, and at the Middle Temple in London. Upon his return to Maryland in 1765 he worked with his father in building up the family fortune. By 1776, when he was 39 years old, he estimated his net worth at 200,000 pounds, and at his death in 1832 his wealth amounted to one and a half million dollars, including 57,000 acres of land, 259 slaves, and silver worth over $6,000. He was a signer of the Declaration of Independence, a state senator, an alderman of Annapolis, and a U.S. senator. He outlived all the other signers and by turning the first spadeful of soil for the Baltimore and Ohio Railway in 1828, bridged the gap between the colonial period and the age of the iron horse.

Maryland State Archives

25

cessful race horse in Maryland, and Tasker sold "Selim" to Samuel Galloway for the record-breaking sum of a thousand pounds.

The purse for the Annapolis races soon became one hundred guineas, a large sum in those days. In the case of special challenges the purse was even more. In 1752, a Maryland mare was taken to Virginia where she beat Alexander Spottswood's "Trial," and enriched her owner by five hundred guineas. Annapolis in its Golden Age was the racing capital of the Chesapeake, and virtually of the thirteen American colonies. The Annapolis Jockey Club, which included some of the wealthiest men in the province, made the September races the social event of the year. A Virginia planter who lived on the Potomac River, Colonel George Washington, visited Annapolis frequently in order to attend the races and other social events, and so did many leading Marylanders.

THANKS to the pleasure-loving tobacco gentry and the tolerance of the Church of England for such innocent pasttimes as dancing, racing, and card-playing (provided they were not carried to excess), Annapolis was receptive to the theatre, and it made an early appearance here. At first, tobacco barns and warehouses were temporarily refitted with makeshift stages for the actors and crude benches for the spectators. In time, permanent theatres were built and traveling companies of players regularly came to town for the season. The first theatre in America that we know of was built in Williamsburg in 1716 and was replaced by a larger one in 1745. The Murray-Kean Company came to Annapolis in 1752 and performed Shakespeare's *Othello* and *Richard III*, as well as such eighteenth-century favorites as *The Provoked Husband, The Lying Valet,* and *The Recruiting Officer.* Another company organized by David Douglass visited Annapolis in 1760 and performed from the beginning of March until the middle of May. They met with such encouragement that they returned to Annapolis each season for the next dozen years. In 1771 a new theatre was erected on West Street not far from St Anne's Church. When completed it drew praise from all sides. An English official new to the area, William Eddis, was agreeably surprised by the stage, the scenery, and the comfortable seats, and favorably compared Douglass's company to the best actors in English provincial theatres of that day.

One of the notable features of life in colonial Annapolis was the number and quality of its gentlemen's clubs. The oldest one in Maryland, the famous South River Club, a few miles south of Annapolis, dates back to 1700 if not earlier and still possesses its "new" clubhouse that was built in 1742. Primarily social, but often with a political or literary bent, clubs sprang up in Annapolis at an early date. Another was the Royalist Club, begun in 1715 by a Scottish Jacobite, George Neilson, who had been transported to the colony for supporting the "Old Pretender" in his unsuccessful bid to wrest the crown from the Hanoverian dynasty. When he was later expelled from the club he founded, he started another, called the Redhouse Club, after the color of its clubhouse. Annapolis also had the Ugly Club, although we can only surmise what the qualifications were for membership! And in 1745, the famous Tuesday Club was founded by another Scotsman, Dr. Alexander Hamilton (1712–1756), who is not to be confused with the later statesman of the same name. Colonial officials, prominent attorneys, physicians, and priests of the Established Church of England—even Jonas Green, the public printer and postmaster of Annapolis, who was also a poet, a punster, and an accomplished punchmaster—rejoiced to belong to it. Like most of the other town clubs, it never owned its own clubhouse. Instead, it met either in the homes of its members or, more commonly, in a local tavern such as the one kept by Samuel Horatio Middleton at the head of the town dock. Voluminous minutes and an illustrated history of the club survive, and they include probably the largest corpus of secular music composed in colonial America. At Tuesday Club meetings, which were frequent, members drank quantities of punch and Madeira; but drinking was purely inci-

Continued on page 30

22 Maryland Avenue. Samuel Chase began this house in 1769 while a young, struggling lawyer who somewhat imprudently married for love rather than money. After the walls were up he ran short of money and sold the unfinished house in 1771 to Colonel Edward Lloyd IV, a wealthy Eastern Shore planter who needed a town house. Lloyd employed an architect, William Buckland (1734–1774), to complete the house and decorate its interior, and it became one of the finest mansions in Annapolis.

Chase-Lloyd House

Samuel Chase (1741–1811) by Sully. Born on the Eastern Shore and educated by his father, an Episcopal priest, Chase became a lawyer, organized the Annapolis "Sons of Liberty," served in the Assembly 1764–1784, was a member of the Continental Congress and a signer of the Declaration of Independence. He influenced Maryland opinion in favor of independence. After the Revolution he was chief judge of the General Court of the State. Although he opposed ratification of the Constitution, he later became a Federalist and in 1796 an associate justice of the U.S. Supreme Court.

Maryland State Archives

Chase-Lloyd House

The entrance hall is demarcated from the stair hall by freestanding Ionic columns, a favorite device of the contemporary British architect, Robert Adam. The stairs rise to a landing, lit by a superb Palladian window, where they divide to form double flanking stairs ascending to the second floor hall.

The second floor hall is distinguished by niches, a delicately designed plaster ceiling, and other classically inspired motifs, and is one of the earliest examples of Adam influence in America.

Being the largest room in the house, this was the scene of festive gatherings, balls, dinners, and other entertainments. It is distinguished by its mahogany doors, marble mantel, and elaborate cornice and chair rail. The portrait between the windows is of the youngest daughter of Colonel Edward Lloyd IV, Mary Tayloe Lloyd, who married Francis Scott Key in this house, and possibly in this room, on January 19, 1802.

The marble mantel in the parlor depicts the immortal Shakespeare receiving keys from the Goddess of Wisdom. Although it does not appear in this photograph, the plaster ceiling of this room, and originally that of the dining room as well, is decorated with intricate Adamesque ornamentation.

dental. Their main purpose was amusement, the pleasure of a cultivated wit. They went in for puns, conundrums, humorous speeches, mock trials, musicmaking, and processions through the streets of the town wearing the club badge and carrying banners. They insisted on avoiding politics and regularly laughed down any member who absent-mindedly introduced such a topic for discussion. The Tuesday Club flourished for over ten years until the death of its founder, Dr. Hamilton. His loss was too much for the other members to bear, and the club soon faded away.

OTHER clubs sprang up in later years: a lodge of Freemasons in 1750, and the Forensic Club in 1769. Unlike most of the other Annapolis clubs, the Forensic Club had a serious purpose and allowed discussion of controversial subjects. Its membership included many rising young lawyers such as Samuel Chase, William Paca, and Thomas Stone, all three of whom later signed the Declaration of Independence. As early as 1761, Paca undertook to debate such issues as "Whether aristocracy be a better form than democracy"; and on another occasion, most remarkable of all was a debate revolving around an even more sensitive subject—the club voted that it was right and proper to "take up arms to deliver subjects from the yoke of a strange prince who is become a tyrant." That, surely, is as treasonable as anything that Patrick Henry said in debating the Stamp Act!

Even during the years of controversy that intervened between the Stamp Act and the Revolution, some Annapolis clubs remained strictly nonpolitical. The Hominy Club, for example, was purely social in the 1770's and devoted itself to innocent merriment; meanwhile, the clouds of disruption were gathering on the horizon. The Tory-minded English priest and rector of St. Anne's Parish, Jonathan Boucher, was its president. Its membership included the governor, Robert Eden, who was later created baronet of Maryland by King George III, as well as leaders of the anti-proprietary or Country party that were soon to become leaders of the movement for American independence.

As the city entered its Golden Age about 1760, there was little to indicate a sudden spurt of prosperity. It was small, boasting no more than perhaps two hundred houses. A few years later, William Eddis, who had come from England to serve as a proprietary official, observed that the town would probably never "attain any importance in a commercial point of view" because "the harbour is not capable of containing many vessels of considerable burthen." But he noticed that many lots were being held for future building and commented that the spirit of improvement was in the air. As a result, he predicted that before long Annapolis would become an impressive city. He proved to be quite correct. During the years 1760 to 1775, the town was virtually transformed by a building boom and became a city of fine houses and gardens with a reputation for a brilliant social life. By 1776, Annapolis had reached its apex of prosperity and elegance, and many of its late colonial structures are still in evidence.

Although never a commercial center comparable to Boston, New York, or Philadelphia, Annapolis had no urban rivals in colonial Maryland in a social sense, and, as we have seen, it was the leading importer of luxury goods. Small as it was, Annapolis was an authentic city in function and the focus of Maryland's political and cultural activities before the Revolution. In later years when the Loyalist, Jonathan Boucher, had returned to his native England and looked back upon the Annapolis he knew in the early 1770's, he could say with enthusiasm and pardonable exaggeration, that it was "the genteelest town in North America," and that "Many of its inhabitants were highly respectable, as to station, fortune and education. I hardly know of a town in England so desirable to live in as Annapolis then was."

There were blacks in Maryland from the very start. One mulatto, Mathias de Sousa, joined the *Ark* in the West Indies and came with the first settlers to Maryland in 1634. He served as an interpreter between the colonists and the Indians, piloted a trading vessel, and was a member of the Gen-

Continued on page 35

William Paca House

Portrait of William Paca (1740–1799) by Charles Willson Peale. Paca was the son of a prosperous planter in what is now Harford County. He was educated at the College of Philadelphia, and studied law at the Middle Temple in London and in Annapolis under Stephen Bordley. He acquired a large fortune by marrying an heiress, was a successful lawyer, and became politically active in the "Country" party. He served in the Continental Congress, signed the Declaration of Independence, and devoted himself wholeheartedly to winning the Revolution. He was a state senator, chief judge of the state, three times governor of Maryland (1782–1785), and a federal district judge (1789–1799).

The Chinese Chippendale bridge and the garden house on the right have been rebuilt to match the view of them in the Peale portrait of William Paca painted in 1772.

William Paca House

186 Prince George Street. The twenty-three year old William Paca began this impressive town house in 1763 just after he married a wealthy heiress, and he lived in it until 1780 when he moved to an even grander mansion on the Eastern Shore.

This room, here set up for dining, has a painted "floor cloth" with a design intended for a marble floor, a great help in decorating a house when there were no operating marble quarries nearby. Paca family silver graces the serving table under the mirror, and Nanking-pattern blue and white porcelain, the dining table.

The bedroom has a cherry chest-on-chest that was made about 1770, the only piece in the house that came from New England. The Prussian blue accents echo the dominant color of the Parlor.

◄
The staircase from the second to the third floor is in Chinese Chippendale style and reflects the "China craze" that well-to-do-Americans caught from their English contemporaries after a trade began in the middle eighteenth century between Great Britain and the Far East. Ninety percent of the original floors survive thanks to the fact that they were carpeted during the years the house served as a hotel. The "Porch Chamber," which is visible in the background, is sunny and bright (weather permitting) and overlooks the garden.

The intricate ornamentation of the overmantel of the restored Parlor did not survive the years when the house was part of Carvel Hall Hotel, but left its "ghosting," thus enabling the recreation of the decoration with a high degree of authenticity. Note the Prussian blue wall paint. Chemical analysis of the first of twenty layers of paint and wallpaper revealed the original paint color, an expensive and fashionable one in the 1760's.

33

William Paca House

The kitchen or herb garden, screened from view by a hedge from the formal garden, had a purely utilitarian purpose.

A popular feature of eighteenth-century Annapolis architecture was the use of galleting, or inserting small pebbles into the mortar in stone foundations. Some people are of the opinion that it was done for decoration only, but others theorize that it had a practical advantage as well, such as strengthening the foundation.

A large wooden hotel known as Carvel Hall was built over the garden in 1907 and demolished in 1965, making possible the restoration of the garden for which the house was celebrated in William Paca's day. Historic Annapolis owns the house. The garden belongs to the State of Maryland. Both are maintained and interpreted to the public by Historic Annapolis.

34

eral Assembly in 1642. Others followed, but after 1664 blacks were generally reduced to slavery. Because slaves provided cheap labor that was much needed on the expanding tobacco plantations, they were in great demand. They were imported in large numbers after 1713, when provisions in the Treaty of Utrecht were favorable to British slave-trading interests. In consequence, they constituted an ever-increasing proportion of the inhabitants of Maryland. In 1704, for example, blacks consisted of only 13% of the population. In the next seventy-five years, despite a large influx of white immigrants, the blacks increased phenomenally and, by the Census of 1790, made up about 33% of the state's inhabitants. Needless to say, they contributed enormously to the economic growth of Maryland.

Until the Revolution most blacks were slaves, and most slaves were laborers. The few who had obtained their freedom and could cope with the English language usually developed skills and became coopers, carpenters, shipwrights, and ferrymen, to name a few of their trades. Because of the nature of slavery and the prejudice against free blacks, very few of them rose high enough to aspire to the learned professions. One of them, however, did so, and in spite of all odds became the first of our black men of science. Benjamin Banneker (1731–1806) was a free black born in Baltimore County who with the help of benevolent Quaker neighbors became a self-educated mathematician and surveyor. Eventually he acquired recognition with the publication of a series of almanacs for Maryland, Virginia, Pennsylvania, and Delaware for the years 1792–1797, that were acknowledged to be more accurate than any others. He is also noted for his letter to Thomas Jefferson in 1791 protesting the injustice of slavery in a nation that rejoiced in liberty. No wonder Jefferson later declared that Banneker's achievements convinced him that blacks were by nature no less intelligent than whites. And when the District of Columbia was surveyed in preparation for laying out the Federal City, Benjamin Banneker served as a scientific assistant.

By the middle of the eighteenth century, as Lord Baltimore's colonial officials sought energetically to raise as large a revenue as possible for Maryland's absentee landlord, opposition arose in the province and consolidated into the "Country party," as opposed to the "Court party," consisting of the Lord Proprietor's officeholders and friends. The spokesmen for the Country party, including Dr. Charles Carroll, Stephen Bordley, William Paca, and Samuel Chase, increasingly reiterated the provision in the royal charter of 1632, in which King Charles I guaranteed to Maryland inhabitants perpetual enjoyment of "all privileges, franchises, and liberties of this our Kingdom of England." When Parliament began to tighten control over the American colonies, the Country party led the opposition in Maryland and ultimately merged with the Patriot parties of the other colonies. But the transition from loyal British subjects seeking redress of colonial grievances to openly rebellious colonists declaring their independence was gradual and did not come to full flower until the winter of 1775–1776.

ALTHOUGH spectacularly successful in the French and Indian War, which greatly enlarged the British Empire by adding Canada and India to it, Britain staggered under an enormous war debt. As a sizable portion of it resulted from British army and navy operations in North America defending the lives and property of the American colonists, the British government undertook to devise new ways of raising revenue in the colonies to help defray the cost of the war. The Stamp Act of 1765 was the first of a series of acts imposing new duties and taxes on the Americans. To the great surprise of the British, the Stamp Act resulted in violent opposition in all the colonies. Here in Maryland Zachariah Hood, who had been appointed the stamp duty collector for the province, was burnt in effigy and some rowdies pulled down Hood's warehouse in Annapolis. Similar episodes occurred in the other colonies as well.

Resistance to the Stamp Act resulted in the for-

McDowell Hall and the Liberty Tree, St. John's College. This well-proportioned building was begun in 1742 when Governor Thomas Bladen secured an appropriation for a new governor's mansion. After the walls were up, but before the roof was added, he ran short of funds and the Assembly declined to vote additional money. For forty years the unfinished structure was known as "Bladen's Folly." In 1784, when St. John's College was chartered, the building was completed for use by the college. The large tulip poplar, known as the "Liberty Tree," is believed to be 400 years old. On hearing news of the Stamp Act in 1765, angry citizens gathered under this tree, then much larger than now, and Samuel Chase and William Paca organized the local "Sons of Liberty" here. In 1840 several mischievous boys discharged some gunpowder in its hollow trunk. Instead of destroying the tree, however, the explosion merely eliminated its parasites and gave it a new lease on life!

mation of the "Sons of Liberty" in virtually every American seaport from Halifax, Nova Scotia, to Savannah, Georgia. Composed mostly of middle-class citizens, the Sons of Liberty coerced stamp distributors into resigning, burned the stamped paper, and incited crowds to attack unpopular local characters. They destroyed property and terrified people in official positions, but to their credit they never actually spilled any blood. Even so, they virtually nullified the Stamp Act. The Annapolis Sons of Liberty, led by Samuel Chase and William Paca, met under the great tulip poplar that stands on St. John's College campus, known to this day as the "Liberty Tree."

American opposition to the new British colonial policy was also carried on through the publication of letters in newspapers up and down the Atlantic coast, and of pamphlets embodying a serious discussion of constitutional principles. One of several important pamphlets at this juncture was written by a prominent resident of Annapolis, Daniel Dulany the Younger, and published by Jonas Green, editor of the *Maryland Gazette*. Dulany's denunciation of the Stamp Act represented a conservative approach. He depicted it as an infringement of the constitutional rights of Americans as British subjects. Because of his familiarity with English history and law, the pamphlet exerted influence in England where it caught the eye of William Pitt. It is credited with being a factor in bringing about the repeal of the hated act the next year.

In stating that Parliament had no right to pass acts "for the single purpose of revenue," but could enact legislation for the regulation of trade, Dulany conceded too much. In an attempt to avoid colonial objections, Parliament passed the Townshend Acts that ostensibly regulated trade and only incidentally raised revenue. Hence, the colonists were obliged to retreat from one position to another. The American position was then reformulated by John Dickinson, a resident of Philadelphia who had been born in Talbot County, Maryland, in his famous "Farmer's Letters." These enunciated the colonists' determination to pay no tax levied by Parliament in any form. Meanwhile, by 1769 local nonimportation agreements up and down the Atlantic coast had reduced British imports into America by nearly one half.

Lord North, who became prime minister in 1770, decided that colonial duties on British manufactures made no sense. With the support of British merchants who exported goods to America, he persuaded Parliament to repeal all the Townshend duties except the one on tea, in order to maintain the principle that Parliament had the right to tax American trade. Colonial trade quickly revived, prosperity returned, and it looked as though Great Britain and America were reconciled.

The radicals in America, however, were determined to keep the quarrel going, and so Samuel Adams engineered the so-called "Boston Tea Party," in which the Sons of Liberty, disguised as

St. John's College, Great Hall. The central chamber of McDowell Hall has been put to many uses over the years. It served as a chapel, an assembly hall, and a ballroom. When Lafayette returned to Annapolis for a visit in 1824, a splendid ball was held here in his honor—certainly one of the most memorable events in the city's three-century history. On its walls hang portraits of many distinguished faculty members, deans, and presidents of the college.

37

Mohawk Indians, dumped 342 chests of tea into the harbor on December 16, 1773. British reaction was prompt and severe, partly because it was the first assault on tea, and partly because it resulted in a large financial loss. There were similar tea parties in other colonies, but these came after the Boston one and were less damaging to British mercantile interests. In Maryland there were tea parties in Annapolis and in Chestertown. On October 15, 1774 the brig *Peggy Stewart* arrived in Annapolis with a cargo including 2,000 pounds of tea. Her owner, Anthony Stewart, after much discussion and many threats prudently ran the vessel aground in Spa Creek and set fire to it with his own hand.

After that, things moved swiftly. Thomas Paine's logic proved effective propaganda and changed many minds in the winter of 1775–1776. On April 6, 1776 the Continental Congress, in defiance of the British navigation acts, declared American trade open to the world. In May it called on each colony to form a state government. Yet Congress hesitated to take the final step. Conservatives hoped that Lord North would make conciliatory offers. But this did not happen. Finally, on June 7, 1776, Richard Henry Lee of Virginia moved in Congress "that these United Colonies are, and of right ought to be, Independent States." Delegates were given time to consult their respective governments. Then, on July 2, 1776, Congress passed Lee's resolution, and two days later the text of the Declaration of Independence was approved. The four signers from Maryland were Charles Carroll of Carrollton, Samuel Chase, William Paca, and Thomas Stone. All four owned houses in Annapolis that are still standing. On the local scene, Maryland formed its state government shortly after independence was voted. The Declaration of Rights and the state Constitution were framed in Annapolis by a committee chaired by Charles Carroll the Barrister. The early governors of Maryland, then chosen by the legislature, were Thomas Johnson (1779–1779), Thomas Sim Lee (1779–1781), and William Paca (1781–1783).

On the eve of the Revolution, Annapolis lost two of its most important public buildings, the sec-

Peggy Stewart House, 207 Hanover Street. Built of all-header bond in the early 1760's, this house was remodeled in 1894 when its original gable roof became a hipped one. In 1774 a Loyalist merchant, Anthony Stewart, acquired the house. On October 14 that year his brig, *Peggy Stewart*, entered Annapolis harbor with a mixed cargo, including some tea in violation of the non-importation agreement. Outraged public opinion and threats of violence forced Stewart to set fire to his vessel—a more spectacular demonstration than the Boston Tea Party (of December 16, 1773), but one which did not injure British merchants as severely. In consequence, Parliament took no retaliatory measures.

ond State House and old St. Anne's Church. Both required extensive repairs and were too small to meet the needs of the growing state and city. Hence they were pulled down to make room for larger and more sophisticated replacements. The old State House was demolished in 1771 and the present one begun the next year. By 1779 it was far enough along for the assembly to meet in it, but the small wooden dome it originally had was later replaced by the present large one in the years 1785–1788. St. Anne's Church was razed in 1775, but the outbreak of the Revolution postponed the erection of its successor until after the war. Meanwhile, services were held in King William's School on State Circle and later in the new theatre until the completion of the second and more elegant St. Anne's Church in 1792.

Portrait of Thomas Stone (1743–1787). In 1781, the house was purchased by Thomas Stone, one of Maryland's four signers of the Declaration of Independence. Of an old Charles County family, Stone studied law under Thomas Johnson (later the first governor of the state) and belonged to the Forensic Club in Annapolis. He also served in the General Assembly and the Continental Congress. Locally, he was recorder of the city of Annapolis and a visitor of St. John's College.

T HE other notable contribution to Annapolis during the Revolution, or rather immediately after it, was the chartering of St. John's College in 1784. The impressive walls of what was to have been the magnificent governor's mansion, begun by Governor Bladen in 1742 and never finished, were given to the college, and the ruin long known as "Bladen's Folly" was completed to house both the faculty and students, the classrooms and library, as well as the dining facilities.

The trustees of King William's School, which had been founded in 1696, voted to turn over the property and endowments of the school to the college and to go out of business as a separate corporation, thus providing St. John's with a claim to be the continuation of an Annapolis institution of learning dating from the seventeenth century. Among American colleges, only Harvard and the College of William and Mary can claim a longer institutional existence.

The war itself greatly affected life in Annapolis. Although threatened several times by British warships in Chesapeake Bay and suffering from prolonged interruption of its customary trade as a result of the Royal Navy's blockade of the Bay,

Annapolis was spared the agony and destruction of an enemy attack. But its brilliant social life was eclipsed by the war and economic hardship deprived even the wealthier inhabitants of their accustomed luxuries.

For the most part, the role of Annapolis during the conflict was to serve as a supply depot. Food, clothing, and weapons were gathered here from all over Maryland and shipped to the armed forces as needed. Newly recruited troops were sent here to be quartered in temporary barracks, awaiting transportation to the war zone.

Annapolis was also the scene of the closing drama of the War for Independence. The Continental Congress met here from November 1783 until August 1784. During those nine months the

Barracks, *43 Pinkney Street.* Just such eighteenth-century "middling" houses as this were commandeered during the Revolution and used to house Continental Army soldiers until they could be shipped to a war zone. Here, during tourist seasons, Historic Annapolis docents interpret Maryland's participation in the War for Independence.

old Senate Chamber in the present State House witnessed two events of national importance. The first was the formal but emotional resignation by General George Washington of his commission as commander-in-chief of the Continental Army. After eight years of war, Washington's efforts had been crowned with success, and at the height of his military fame and national popularity he gave back his commission to the civil authorities. On December 23, 1783, like Cincinnatus of old, he returned to his home and family, little supposing that the nation he helped to bring to birth would call upon him in the future to be its first president.

The State House also witnessed, on January 14,

1784, the formal ratification of the Treaty of Paris, which in the drama of the American Revolution ranks in significance with the Declaration of Independence. Scholars consider it to be the most important treaty ever negotiated by the United States. The founding fathers secured British acquiescence to our independence so bravely declared in 1776, a vast new territory, and international recognition.

Yet another notable event occurred in Annapolis. After the war, the American states suffered inflation and hard times that caused political and economic instability, including debtor uprisings like Shays' Rebellion in Massachusetts, and a mutual levying of duties on interstate commerce. Merchants and other men of property were alarmed. In 1785, the Virginia Assembly invited the states to send delegates to Annapolis the next year "to take into consideration the trade of the United States." Meeting in Mann's Tavern on Conduit Street, the Annapolis convention of 1786 was so poorly attended that two of its younger members, Alexander Hamilton and James Madison, convinced the others that nothing could be done unless all the states were represented. In the report written by Hamilton the critical situation of confederation was emphasized and a proposal made that all thirteen states send delegates to a convention "to devise such further provisions as shall appear to them necessary to render the constitution of the federal government adequate to the exigencies of the Union." The appeal that went out from Annapolis proved to be the genesis of the Constitutional Convention that met in Philadelphia in 1787. Their deliberations produced the Constitution under which our fifty United States still live.

But ratification was not a foregone conclusion. There was a great deal of opposition, especially in the larger states. In Maryland, however, an overwhelming majority favored it. Even so, those few who opposed it were men of stature articulate enough to be able to influence others. Among the foremost of the Maryland antifederalists was the former governor, William Paca, who like Patrick Henry in Virginia, had been a staunch patriot in the War for Independence but opposed the Constitution

Maryland Hall of Records

This watercolor, done about 1794, and now in the Hammond-Harwood House, enables us to imagine what it would be like to step back into the town at that time. What is now the Maryland Inn appears here in its original, Georgian guise, rather than in the Victorian one given it after the Civil War.

Maryland Inn, *Church Circle between Main and Duke of Gloucester Streets.* In 1772 the builder announced in the *Maryland Gazette* that he was erecting "an elegant brick house," 100 feet long, three stories high, with twenty rooms and fireplaces. It was the first structure in Annapolis designed to be a hotel, and not just a house that could serve interchangeably as a residence, a shop, or a tavern. In 1784 it was called the "King of France Tavern," in gratitude for the help given by Louis XVI in winning our independence and in deference to the French soldiers quartered in Annapolis. Enlarged and modernized in 1868, it acquired such Victorian features as a mansard roof and porches, which disguise its eighteenth-century origin. It still serves as one of the leading hotels in Annapolis. The Price House, mentioned on page 48, is visible across Main Street, the second building from the left.

Mann's Tavern, *Conduit Street.* Towards the end of the Revolution, Colonel George Mann bought this confiscated Tory property from the State and operated his famous inn here and on adjacent lots. General Washington put up at Mann's Hotel in 1783 when he resigned his commission as commander of the Continental Army, and the Annapolis Convention of 1786 that was the immediate precursor of Philadelphia's Constitutional Convention of 1787 also met at Mann's. Today, the handsome eighteenth-century building is the Masonic Hall. In the 1830's a later owner built a brick addition that extended to the Duke of Gloucester Street. After it was subdivided in 1910 into six private dwellings, it has come to be known as "Rainbow Row," because of the variety of colors they have been painted.

on the grounds that it did not specifically protect the civil rights of individuals. Paca, however, was persuaded by the Federalist leaders to suspend his public opposition in return for their promise that a bill of rights would be added as soon as the new congress met. This afforded Paca the opportunity to make specific proposals for improving the document while avoiding the appearance of being dead-set against it. As the eyes of the Virginians were upon the proceedings in Annapolis, Maryland's almost unanimous ratification helped tip the balance in Virginia, where it was bitterly contested and the outcome uncertain, and therefore facilitated the launching of the Constitution on its career. Paca's specific proposals for correcting the defects of the document, moreover, helped prepare the way for adding the first ten amendments, or Bill of Rights.

After the war it became increasingly clear that the Golden Age of Annapolis was fading. In the 1780's the city was one of several in the country that were considered for the national capital. Although disappointed in that hope, Annapolitans derived comfort from the fact that their city remained the capital of Maryland despite the near success of Baltimore's bid for that distinction in 1786. Her commerce, however, and to a large extent her wealth and social preeminence, shifted to Baltimore, which had become the Queen of the Chesapeake, the largest city and port in Maryland.

Although many of the first families of Annapolis moved to Baltimore after the Revolution, those who remained perpetuated on a reduced scale the genteel tradition for which the city had been noted. And Annapolis was able to claim several nationally known citizens in the period between the Revolution and the Civil War.

The celebrated statesman, William Pinkney (1764–1822), was born in Annapolis and educated at King William's School. He later served in Congress, became a senator, and was minister to Great Britain, to the Kingdom of Naples, and to Russia. His brilliant interpretation of the Constitution, strengthened by his oratory, contributed to the passage of the Missouri Compromise of 1820. Other members of the Annapolis Pinkneys were

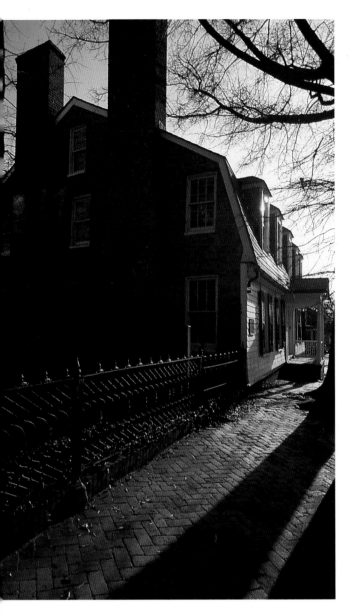

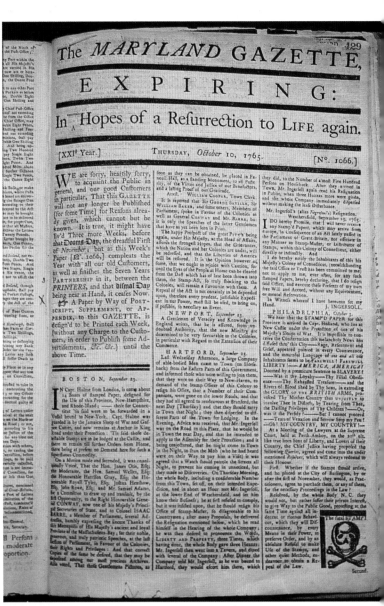

Jonas Green House, *124 Charles Street.* After 1738 this early eighteenth-century gambrel-roofed house was the home and print shop of Jonas Green, a printer, poet, convivial clubmember, and an acute observer of political life who published the *Maryland Gazette* from 1745 until his death in 1767. Later his widow, Anne Catherine Green, continued his business and served as the official printer of the province. Their sons Frederick and Samuel kept the paper going until it was sold in the 1840's. The house has remained in the possession of their descendants to this day.

Here is the front page of Jonas Green's own copy of the *Maryland Gazette* for October 10, 1765, showing evidence of colonial mourning for the potential deathblow given the press by the heavy tax levied by the detested Stamp Act.

Archaeological excavation in recent years has turned up this cut of a death's head which Jonas Green had made for the issue of the *Maryland Gazette* in which he deplored the effects of the Stamp Act on the colonial press.

East Street at Prince George. This impressive, five-part Georgian mansion with its massive chimneys rising 60 feet above the street level would be appropriate on a thousand-acre plantation, yet it was built in a town and has virtually no land around it. Young James Brice, the son of John Brice II and brother of John Brice III, built this house in 1767–1774.

James Brice House

The handsome staircase and plaster molding give the visitor a clue to the high quality of work that was being done in Annapolis on the eve of the Revolution.

The parlor is one of the most intricately decorated rooms of colonial America. It is purposely shown without furnishings in order to avoid distracting the visitor's attention from the superb ornamentation.

Famous for its beautiful plaster and woodwork, this house was purchased in 1982 by the International Union of Bricklayers and Allied Craftsmen.

Ninian, who owned the Hammond-Harwood House in 1810; Ninian, Jr., who was Medical Director of the U.S. Navy; and another William, who was the Episcopal Bishop of Maryland, 1870–1883.

The other great American statesman who came from Annapolis was Reverdy Johnson (1796–1876), who was born in the Bordley-Randall House and educated at St. John's College. He was the chief counsel in the famous Dred Scott Case in 1856. Although he considered slavery to be wrong, he thought it proper to protect the legal rights of slaveholders until such time as slavery could be constitutionally ended. His arguments greatly influenced the Supreme Court's decision, rendered by another Marylander, Chief Justice Roger Brooke Taney. Again, although a lifelong Democrat, Johnson supported Lincoln when it came to secession. After the war, as a senator, he fought against the Republican Radicals and strove to give decent treatment to the fallen South. In 1868, although handicapped by partial blindness, he served as minister to Great Britain where his conciliatory negotiations paved the way for the settlement of the *Alabama* claims.

Another person dear to the hearts of Annapolitans, although not well known throughout the nation, was Dr. John Ridgely. In the war with Tripoli in 1804, Ridgely, who was a naval surgeon, was captured along with other Americans aboard the USS *Philadelphia* and held for ransom. When the children of the Bashaw of Tripoli took ill, Dr. Ridgely was summoned to attend them. Upon their recovery, the grateful bashaw is said to have offered the hand of his daughter in marriage. Having a fiancee at home, the doctor politely declined the honor, but accepted several gifts including a fine Arabian horse which he brought back with him to Annapolis.

Perhaps most famous of all was the author of our national anthem, Francis Scott Key (1779–1843). Although he was not born here and lived most of his life elsewhere, he has so many associations with the city that Annapolitans consider him one of their own. While a student at St. John's grammar school and college, 1779–1796, he lived

Continued on page 48

Ridout House

120 Duke of Gloucester Street. When Horatio Sharpe came to Maryland as governor in 1753, he brought as his secretary a young Oxford graduate, John Ridout. Under the governor's patronage, Ridout received lucrative appointments in the province and in 1764 married Mary, the daughter of the former governor, Samuel Ogle. Soon afterwards he built this splendid house which has belonged to his descendants ever since. Like several other Annapolis houses, it is built in all-header bond, a popular feature in this area in the middle eighteenth century, and something of a rarity elsewhere.

The archway which frames the staircase springs from a handsomely scrolled bracket.

Unique in Annapolis, this colorful garland of painted red roses was discovered recently under layers of paint on the mantelpiece.

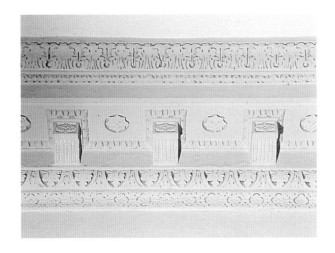

This molded cornice features a rosette between modillions trimmed with egg and dart bands. Ornate plasterwork cast in classical orders was popular in Annapolis during its Golden Age. Skilled plasterers advertised their wares in the *Maryland Gazette,* and the demand seems to have kept up with the supply.

Garden Front. The most notable features are the Palladian window, one of the earliest in Maryland, and the way in which the roofline was modified to accommodate it.

with his aunt at the Upton Scott House. He also studied law here with his uncle, Philip Barton Key, in the College Avenue wing of the Bordley-Randall House. And in 1802 he married a daughter of Colonel Edward Lloyd IV in the Chase-Lloyd House. He also founded the Alumni Society of St. John's College, and the auditorium of the college is named for him.

In the years of its decline during the early nineteenth century, Annapolis lost a number of its colonial buildings, some to fires and others to remodeling in later styles. A disastrous fire in 1790, for example, destroyed most of the buildings along the west side of the dock, and new ones arose to take their places. The buildings on the north side, now 26–28 Market Space, which housed the mercantile activities of the leading late colonial and early post-Revolutionary merchants of Annapolis—Wallace, Davidson, and Johnson—were devastated by fire much later. They were rebuilt incorporating the walls of the 1772 building, but with a different facade. Others, like 10 Francis Street, the Maryland Inn, and old St. Anne's Rectory on Hanover Street, were given modern facades or mansard roofs, thereby partially concealing their colonial origins.

Attempts were made to deepen the harbor and make Annapolis the seaport for the national capital. Nothing came of them except that incoming foreign diplomats often disembarked at Annapolis, preferring the short overland stagecoach ride to the tortuous, hundred-mile trip up the winding Potomac River to Washington—at least until steamships replaced sailing vessels. Annapolis was also used by Northern congressmen and others who crossed Chesapeake Bay in sailing ferries. For the most part, however, in the decades before the Civil War, the residents of Annapolis devoted themselves to improving their city rather than trying to regain their departed glory. By-laws in 1832 required hogs to be kept in pens. The principal streets were paved for the first time, and provided with brick sidewalks and street lamps. Public pumps were maintained for the convenience of the inhabitants and to furnish water for the town fire engines.

In 1838, the City of Annapolis collected $4,500 in property taxes, which amounted to 87 1/2 cents per $100, and included wharfage, licenses on carriages and carts, and income from the Market House. Expenditures that year amounted to $3,000, including the cost of employing constables "to visit those parts of the city which most require their presence every night . . . to preserve the lamps and other property." That left a surplus of some $1,500, or one-third for other than routine expenses, which good fortune many hard-pressed, twentieth-century mayors must envy!

Until the last decade or two of the eighteenth century, many Annapolis blacks remained in legal bondage, but after the Revolution slave manumissions multiplied, partly as a result of the aggressive stand of Quakers and the early Methodists against slavery. By 1800 there were more free blacks in Maryland than in any other state in the Union. By law, slaves could not be freed unless they were able to support themselves. Hence, many free black Annapolitans ran small shops or earned their living as carpenters, drayers, or shoemakers, and before long they began to acquire property. Among the early free blacks were several who were progenitors of families that have been a part of life of the city ever since. One of these, Smith Price, a former slave of the prominent planter Daniel of St. Thomas Jenifer, owned quite a bit of land in and near the city. In 1803 he sold a lot just beyond the city gate on West Street to the newly organized African Methodist Episcopal Church. Other prominent black families that got their start in business and land-owning before the Civil War were the Bishops, the Shorters, and the Butlers. In 1835 Henry Price, son of Smith Price, built what is now 230–236 Main Street, which he and his descendants owned for many years. Price became a preacher in the A.M.E. Church and was greatly respected as a civic and religious leader in Annapolis. About 1840 another free black tradesman, Henry Matthews, owned the house that is now 176 Main Street. It was built by another black, Charles Shorter, who also erected an earlier building for what is now the Asbury Methodist Church, and he served as the first superintendent of

4 Shipwright Street. Another product of the Golden Age of Annapolis, this impressive house was built in 1762-65 by Dr. Upton Scott, a Northern Irish physician who had come to Maryland in 1753 with Governor Horatio Sharpe. Like John Ridout who came at the same time, Scott received lucrative public offices under the patronage of the governor. The last colonial governor of Maryland, Sir Robert Eden, an ancestor of Anthony Eden, Earl of Avon, died while visiting Dr. Scott after the Revolution, and his mortal remains are now in St. Anne's Churchyard. Later, Mrs. Scott's nephew, Francis Scott Key, author of our national anthem, lived here while a student at St. John's College from which he was graduated in 1796 at the age of seventeen.

Upton Scott House

Paneled like the parlor, the dining room is distinguished by an equally fine mantel carved with a wall-of-Troy design like that on the front door and staircase. The handsome door just beyond the fireplace which originally was a china cupboard, now leads to a modern kitchen.

49

Upton Scott House

A view of the graceful staircase and front door framed by an arch of pleasing proportions supported by pilasters.

Stair detail.

The fine plaster paneling and handsome fireplace make the parlor as desirable a room today as it was in Dr. Scott's day. The brackets on the mantel echo those on the outside cornice of the house. The fireplace has a fireback dated 1765 and made by the Patuxent Iron Works in nearby Prince George's County.

its Sunday school. A free black couple, John and Lucy Smith, occupied the charming colonial brick house at 160 Prince George Street before the Civil War. John Smith was a "drayer" or hauler, and ran a livery stable. His wife, known as "Aunt Lucy," was a noted cook and ran a catering business. Among her customers were some of the leaders of Annapolis society, including several governors of Maryland.

ONE of the most significant events in Annapolis during the first half of the nineteenth century was the founding of the United States Naval Academy in 1845. After a British warship attacked the USS *Chesapeake* off the Virginia capes in 1808, war seemed imminent, and in anticipation of trouble the Federal government built Fort Severn on the point where the Naval Academy now stands. Its presence may have saved Annapolis from attack during the War of 1812. Several Royal Navy squadrons anchored in the mouth of the Severn River, but none bombarded the city.

Fort Severn continued to be garrisoned until 1845, when the Secretary of the Navy, George Bancroft, persuaded the War Department to transfer it to the Navy so that he might establish the new naval school he was planning. From that small beginning grew the impressive United States Naval Academy, which has been a major factor in the life of Annapolis ever since—except for the Civil War years when it was moved to Newport, Rhode Island, to protect it from the Southern sympathies and pro-Confederate proclivities of many Annapolitans.

In the presidential election of 1860, Abraham Lincoln got only one vote in Annapolis, and only three in Anne Arundel County. By tradition and sentiment, Annapolis was a part and parcel of the Old South. For that reason, among others, when the Civil War was precipitated by the firing on Fort Sumter, President Lincoln took prompt and decisive action to prevent Maryland from seceding. Had that happened, the Federal capital would have been in the Confederacy and the Northern states might appear in European eyes to be the insurgents. Northern regiments were sent to Baltimore where the guns of Fort McHenry were turned on the city. The pro-Union governor summoned the General Assembly to meet, not in Annapolis, but in Frederick, far removed from Confederate sympathizers. Lincoln also suspended the Writ of Habeas Corpus and summarily imprisoned many southern Maryland leaders who were thought to be secessionists. The Secretary of the Navy quickly moved the Naval Academy to Rhode Island, and Annapolis was occupied in 1861 by Massachusetts and New York regiments under the notorious General Ben Butler. Although he met with no overt acts of resistance, a Palmetto flag (the symbol of South Carolina) was displayed at St. Anne's Church. It was quickly removed, but on another occasion a Confederate flag was flown elsewhere in town until spotted by the occupation forces.

No military action occurred here, but Annapolis witnessed large numbers of wounded soldiers brought to the Union hospital set up at St. John's College and on the grounds of the Naval Academy. An even larger number of paroled captives returned by the Confederates were housed and processed at a camp several miles west of the town at a place ever since called Parole. The city also witnessed the drinking and gambling parties of the 53rd New York Infantry, known as D'Epeneuil's Zouaves, whose colorful uniforms consisted of baggy blue trousers, blue coats with yellow facings, yellow leggings, and red caps with yellow tassels. The War between the States was a time of quiet desperation for the many pro-Confederates of Annapolis. Even after the war, there was doubt about the wisdom of returning the Naval Academy to Annapolis where the midshipmen might be exposed to disaffected Annapolitans of Southern sentiment. But the Maryland Congressional delegation, supported by the governor, carried the day and Congress authorized the return of the Naval Academy to its former home.

The freeing of the slaves in 1865 opened new opportunities to Maryland blacks. One of the early black businessmen of Annapolis, William H. But-

Continued on page 58

Naval Academy Yard. In the foreground is the Mexican War monument, commemorating the four Naval Academy graduates who lost their lives in naval operations at Vera Cruz in 1846–1847, and erected in 1848 by the alumni and midshipmen of the Academy. Beyond it can be seen the back of Tecumseh, a bronze statue of an Indian, a copy of the wooden figurehead of the 74-gun USS *Delaware*, built in 1820, and salvaged in 1868. To protect it from the elements, the old figurehead is now kept in the Halsey Field House. The bronze replica has stood on its former site since 1930. In the background is Bancroft Hall, which is the dormitory for midshipmen—all 4,500 of them—and one of the largest buildings of its kind in the world.

Memorial Hall, Bancroft Hall. This splendid hall, with its parquet floor, crystal chandeliers, and view of Chesapeake Bay, is a memorial to all the graduates of the Naval Academy who have given their lives for their country since the institution was established in 1845. Ernest Flagg (1857–1947), who studied at the Ecole des Beaux Arts in Paris, was commissioned in 1899 to rebuild the Academy, and he was responsible for designing Bancroft Hall, the Chapel, and the old academic complex, including Mahan, Maury, and Sampson halls.

Superintendent's House.
The formal dining room is distinguished by its fine Waterford crystal chandelier, a French Empire dining table, which has fourteen leaves and can seat twenty-four guests, and a mahogany sideboard that was used in the captain's cabin aboard USS *Constitution* ("Old Ironsides") until 1855 when it was transferred to the Naval Academy. The Asher B. Durand portrait of Washington has belonged to the Academy since 1892.

U.S. Naval Academy photograph

The Naval Academy

The new Academy buildings form a backdrop for the midshipmen's sailboats with their colorful spinnakers—a familiar sight in the Severn River on good days. From right to left are the Nimitz Library, named for the famous World War II admiral; Rickover Hall for the "Father of the Nuclear Navy," and Chauvenet and Michelson Halls named for two early professors at the Academy. The former was instrumental in founding the Academy and served on the original seven-man faculty in 1845. The second was an Academy graduate who as an ensign successfully measured the speed of light in 1878 and later became the first American scientist to win a Nobel Prize.

The Naval Academy

The meticulously maintained Academy grounds reflect the seasons of the year and are freely open to visitors. Because of its enlightened policy of hospitality, the Academy is closely associated in the minds of Annapolitans with their city and is greatly enjoyed by them. The doors of the chapel were designed in 1902 by a young woman sculptor, Evelyn Beatrice Longman (1874–1954), who won the competition for the best design. The wealthy donor then sent her abroad for a year to learn the technique of working a mold for casting. The doors, which were completed in 1908, are ten feet wide and have a total height with the transom of twenty-two feet.

The Chapel. The stained-glass windows in the apse and transepts commemorate such
naval heroes as Sampson, Porter, and Farragut. Its crypt contains the mortal remains of
John Paul Jones in a setting that is almost as grand as that of Napoleon Bonaparte in Paris.

ler, bought an impressive town house at 148 Duke of Gloucester Street in 1863, and it remained in his family until 1922. He became the first black alderman of the City of Annapolis in 1873—and, indeed, the first black elected official in the State. His son, William H. Butler, Jr., served on the City Council 1893–1897. Despite the Southern sentiment during the Civil War, there have been no fewer than eighteen black aldermen in Annapolis, one of whom served as acting mayor of Annapolis in 1981.

Since the Civil War more and more blacks have entered the learned professions. Dr. Daniel Hale Williams (1856–1931), who was a grandson of Henry Price and who lived in the Price House on Main Street in his later years, performed one of the world's earliest successful heart operations. In 1893 he sutured the pericardium of a stabbing victim and the patient recovered. In 1902 another black physician, Dr. William Bishop, was one of the founders of the Anne Arundel General Hospital, the charter of which declared that it was for "white and colored patients." Dr. Bishop lived at 14 Church Circle where the Maryland National Bank now stands.

Among the most interesting of Annapolis blacks was the late Wiley H. Bates, a coal merchant, storekeeper, philanthropist, and political leader. Born a slave in 1858, he worked his way up the ladder of success by force of character and hard work. After working on the railroad, as a waiter, and as an oysterman, he boldly opened his own shop on Cathedral and South streets at a time when he had only twelve cents in his pocket. Ultimately, however, he made enough money to help build and furnish the public school that was later named for him. He bequeathed to the school and to the town an impressive standard of excellence which bore fruit in many young people of later generations.

The response of the community to the new interest in black history is seen in the preservation of the former Mount Moriah African Methodist Church, 84 Franklin Street. Built nearly a century before, it was taken over by the county in 1971 and scheduled to be torn down to make room for a

Old Mount Moriah Church,
84 Franklin Street. A group of blacks formed a church in Annapolis about 1799 which was chartered in 1803 and later became affiliated with the African M.E. Church. Erected about 1876, this Victorian Gothic Revival building was Mount Moriah Church for nearly a century, when a new and larger one was built elsewhere. The old building has been restored and is the Banneker-Douglass Museum of Afro-American History and Culture.

parking lot. At that juncture, Historic Annapolis and others, together with the Maryland Commission on Afro-American History and Culture, intervened, secured its recognition as a historic building, and blocked its demolition by court action. Thus saved, the building has since been handsomely restored by action of the State, and converted into the Banneker-Douglass Museum, named for Maryland's eighteenth-century surveyor and almanac maker, Benjamin Banneker, and for Frederick Douglass, her nineteenth-century abolitionist, orator, journalist, and diplomat. The first state-owned museum of Afro-American history and culture in the country, it puts on changing exhibits, serves as a focal point of activities relating to black history, and extends its influence throughout Maryland by means of conferences, publications, and traveling exhibits.

The conspicuous success of the American navy in the Spanish-American War of 1898 conferred new lustre on our naval prestige, and when Theodore Roosevelt, who had long favored a stronger navy, entered the White House, the Academy was greatly enlarged and completely rebuilt. Several city blocks were taken over and added to the Academy's grounds. The displaced inhabitants were relocated by building additional houses on small lots between existing structures and on what were formerly gardens and vacant lots. Together with its growth in population, this transformed the old city from one of spacious lots, much grass, and many trees, into its present urban appearance. It also led to the building of new bridges over the creeks that almost surround the old city and to the spilling of the population into the surrounding countryside. Indeed, so many Annapolitans eventually lived across Spa, College, and Weems creeks, that in the 1950's its boundary was greatly enlarged and its environs incorporated into the city proper. The twentieth century has witnessed the old city's transformation into a modern one, connected by high-speed highways to both Baltimore and Washington, and provided with easy access to the Eastern Shore by the construction of the Chesapeake Bay Bridge in 1952, enlarged by a second span in 1973. New apartment complexes

have arisen, as well as town houses and condominiums, attracting commuters who work in the two nearby metropolises. The other notable development has been the tragic decline of oystering and the Bay fisheries, and the rise of Annapolis as a center for yachting, now its largest "industry" other than government, education, and the tourist trade. As the years melted into centuries and new fashions succeeded one another, the newer buildings of Annapolis have reflected the progression of styles, and the city has become a veritable outdoor museum of American architectural taste from the late seventeenth century to the present. In addition to more than one hundred eighteenth-century survivals, Annapolis can show visitors examples of Federal style, Classic, Romanesque, and Gothic revival, and Queen Anne style architecture. In addition, the Naval Academy constitutes an unsurpassed aggregation of buildings in the Beaux Arts classic style for which the architect, Ernest Flagg, is celebrated. Last but not least there are also examples of contemporary architecture, notably the Harbormaster's House on the City Dock, the Farmers National Bank on lower Main Street, and Mellon Hall at St John's College.

BEFORE Annapolis entered its renewed prosperity, however, it went through a lean period when its obsolescence led some entrepreneurs to believe that the only way to revitalize it was to redevelop it like inner cities up and down the coast. In consequence, pressure was exerted to replace deteriorating buildings by new and larger ones, thus threatening to change the character of the old city. This gave rise to the preservation movement that mercifully has saved historic Annapolis. Some old houses had been preserved by their owners. Others were saved by local institutions, such as St. John's College and the U.S. Naval Academy Alumni Association. The Library Association saved Reynolds Tavern. The Chase-Lloyd House was preserved because it was bequeathed in 1886 to a trust composed of Maryland Episcopalians,

Continued on page 62

Acton Place, *Franklin Street.* Taking its name from Richard Acton, to whom Cecil, Lord Baltimore, made a land grant in 1651, this fine house was built by Phillip Hammond before the Revolution and is distinguished by its broad chimneys that parallel the facade. When built, it was a plantation house in the country, but Annapolis now has grown and encompassed it.

Adams Kilty House, *131 Charles Street.* The two massive chimneys facing forward remind one of Acton Place and are, perhaps, the most striking feature of this late eighteenth-century town house other than its stark simplicity. It takes its name from William Adams, an Eastern Shore planter who owned the property in 1773, and William Kilty who made it his home in 1779. A surgeon turned lawyer, Kilty compiled The Laws of Maryland, Annapolis, 1799, and was Chancellor of the State, 1806–1821.

City Dock. The red brick building to the left (77 Main Street) is called the Victualling Warehouse. During the Revolution the State confiscated this property which belonged to a Loyalist and used his warehouse as a collection center for food and supplies for the Continental Army. The restored building belongs to the State and now houses a museum operated by Historic Annapolis which depicts the maritime aspects of Annapolis in the second half of the eighteenth century.

Cornhill Street, *off State Circle.* In 1769 a prominent merchant, Charles Wallace, purchased a tract of undeveloped land between State Circle and the Town Dock and laid out two new streets, Cornhill and Fleet, named for celebrated London thoroughfares. This picturesque street was occupied in the late eighteenth century by Annapolitans of the "middling sort"; number 49 belonged to William Monroe, a carpenter, and Number 53 to Thomas Callahan, a tailor. Numbers 37-39, originally one building, housed John Brewer's Tavern where Thomas Jefferson placed his groom and horses during the session of the Continental Congress in Annapolis, 1783-1784. (Jefferson himself put up at Mrs. Ghiselins's on West Street where the cuisine was more to his liking.) Brewer's niece, Rachel, while a serving girl here, met the painter Charles Willson Peale and became his wife.

headed ex officio by the Bishop of Maryland. Meanwhile, the College, St. Anne's, and St. Mary's preserved their own historic buildings, and the State of Maryland did the same for the State House and the Old Treasury Building. But other notable edifices in the town were threatened. At one time Henry Ford was considering buying the Hammond-Harwood House and moving it brick by brick to Michigan, and no one knew what would happen to the James Brice House. Fortunately the Hammond-Harwood Association was organized in 1938. It purchased the splendid Georgian mansion, and keeps it open to the public. The Brice House was acquired in 1953 by a private owner who

restored and preserved it, and after his death it was bought by the International Union of Bricklayers and Allied Craftsmen to be a museum. The handsome late eighteenth-century brick building at the corner of Main and Green streets traditionally known as the Old Custom House was rescued from demolition in 1957 by a group of individuals who became incorporated under the name Port of Annapolis, Inc.

The first attempt to create a nonprofit corporation devoted to saving the historic area as a whole was in 1935 when the Company for the Restoration of Colonial Annapolis came into being. Although it rendered a great service by calling attention to the need, its plan for moving historic structures from their original sites to the waterfront came to nothing and the organization dissolved in controversy in the mid-1940's. Indeed, public apathy and conflicting interests of various competing parties contributed to the demise of several early preservation organizations. Meanwhile, commercial interests and thoughtless attempts by uninformed owners to modernize their buildings continued to play havoc with the architectural heritage of Annapolis. Then, in 1952, Historic Annapolis, Inc. was founded, and it has succeeded where its predecessors failed.

Its success, however, was not instantaneous, for it inherited all the difficulties of its predecessors. But the extraordinary determination of its handful of dedicated members enabled it to survive, and in due course, to create a new and changed atmosphere in Annapolis that is conducive to historic preservation. By vigorous advocacy the new organization countered the notion that Annapolis was an unattractive, outmoded town unable to draw vis-

itors and destined to lose its historic resources. And by offering an innovative plan of creative preservation, it translated dreams into action and brought about an incredible transformation.

Historic Annapolis set about to combine public and private funds to restore and preserve not only buildings but also the historic quality of the Annapolis environment, and to improve the economic stability of this small but nationally important city. Although adequate funding has never been available, the plan has already regenerated an urban quality once obliterated by decay and mutilation. Priority was given to a study of the factors which give Annapolis its special character. Techniques for preserving the area were developed after evaluating programs used elsewhere. Donations were obtained to finance historic and environmental research, to buy historic buildings, to purchase "easements," or restrictive clauses in property conveyances to prevent alteration or destruction of architectural features, and to establish a revolving fund. Unlike Colonial Williamsburg, which is

Charles Carroll the Barrister House, *St. John's College.* Dr. Charles Carroll (1691–1755), the patriarch of the Episcopal Carrolls, came to Annapolis from Ireland about 1715 and accumulated a fortune as a merchant, planter, shipbuilder, and investor in the Baltimore Iron Works. He built this house about 1723 and his more famous son, known as "The Barrister," was presumably born in it. Charles Carroll the Barrister (1723–1783) became a leading patriot in Revolutionary Maryland. To save the house from demolition, Historic Annapolis moved it in 1955 to St. John's College campus from its original location at the corner of Main and Conduit streets.

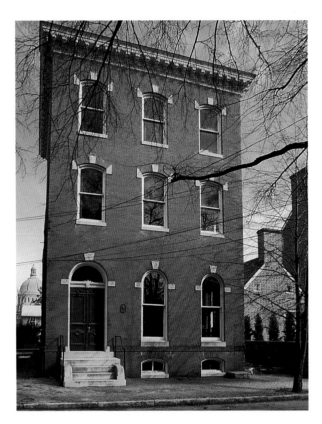

Gassaway-Feldmeyer House, *194 Prince George Street.* This is a good example of a mid-Victorian merchant's sumptuous town house. Built about 1870, it now serves as the headquarters of Historic Annapolis and is gradually being restored and furnished appropriately.

largely professional, Historic Annapolis carries on its activities largely through the good offices of volunteers, augmented by a small but competent staff and occasional outside professional consultants. With a small operating budget, it has nonetheless saved some thirty historically and architecturally important structures in Annapolis, and it has been instrumental in saving no fewer than three hundred others. Much of its operating budget comes from small annual contributions from its 3,000 members, from tours and special events, sales of publications, and fees from preservation consultations conducted by its staff and officers. Special fund-raising drives are held to purchase, restore, and furnish museum buildings, and Historic Annapolis has received Federal, State, and County grants. It also maintains a revolving fund of approximately $200,000 used to purchase properties endangered by neglect, demolition, or adverse use. Once such buildings have been saved, they are sold to sympathetic owners who agree to restore them according to plans provided by Historic Annapolis with easements designed to protect them in the future. The sale price is then returned to the revolving fund to be used over and over again. So far, some seventy structures have been bought and sold in this way. In order to assist private owners who are interested in restoring their properties, Historic Annapolis maintains a Preservation Data Bank which is available not only to owners but also to architects, planners, government agencies, and journalists.

Sometimes to save a house from demolition, it must be moved to another site. Historic Annapolis has raised funds or coordinated fund-raising to save two notable colonial buildings from destruction: the Charles Carroll Barrister House, now on the campus of St. John's College, and the Callahan-Pinkney House now on Conduit Street. On another occasion it saved the Paca House by purchasing and restoring it when it was scheduled to be torn down to make way for a modern high-rise. It now owns several other buildings that are awaiting funds for restoration.

Early in the 1960's, commercial developers devised a plan for a high-rise hotel, over eighty feet in height, to be built in the Market Space. Historic Annapolis responded to the challenge and was responsible for defeating the proposal. It also persuaded the city to change its building code to prevent such anomalies in the future. Finally, in 1965 the historic District of Annapolis was officially designated a National Historic Landmark District by the Secretary of the Interior, Stewart Udall, and this was given legal support by the inhabitants of Annapolis in 1969, when they voted two-to-one in all eight wards of the city to establish the Annapolis District Ordinance.

Much remains to be done, particularly in raising more funds for restoration, but the war on decay and apathy has been won and Historic Annapolis has saved the ancient city for the future.   ✣

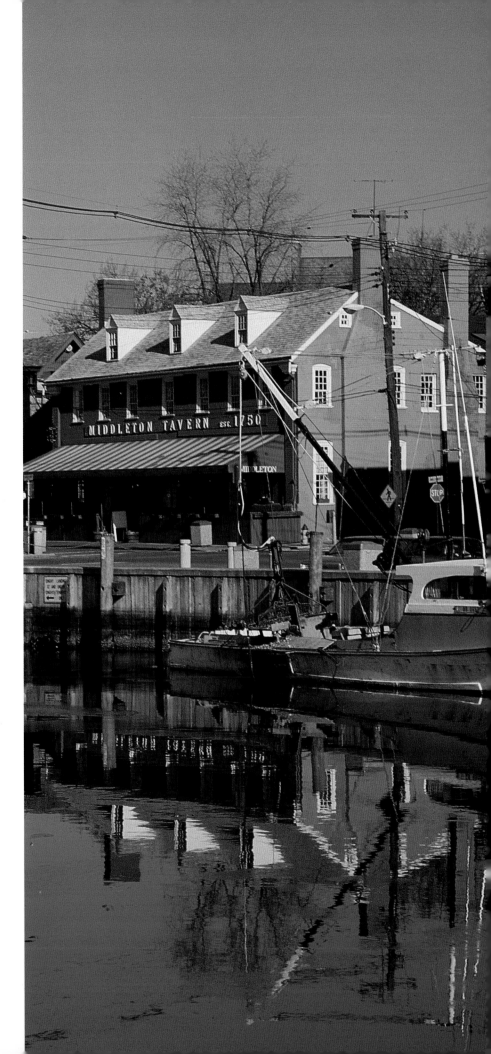

Middleton's Tavern, *at the head of the City Dock.* From about 1740 until the Revolution, Samuel Horatio Middleton and his son kept a tavern in this building. Here the famous Tuesday Club, the Jockey Club, and others often met. Visiting dignitaries were treated to a glass of wine here as they came ashore at the landing. Here, too, the clergy of the Established (i.e., Episcopal) Church met periodically in convocations. The Middletons also operated a sailing ferry from Annapolis to Rock Hall on the Eastern Shore which shortened the overland route to Philadelphia by thirty miles. After the Revolution the tavern was refitted as a merchant's establishment.

Reynolds' Tavern, *Church Circle*. William Reynolds, a hatter, built this house about 1747 as a residence and place of business. During periods of war with France when the tobacco trade was disrupted and the sale of fine hats fell off, Reynolds operated a tavern here which acquired a good reputation. Like a number of other colonial Annapolis houses, this one is built in all-header bond, a rarity elsewhere but a common occurrence in tidewater Maryland in the eighteenth century.

Dock Street. At the right is part of the Market House, built in 1858, restored in 1972, and still serving its original purpose. The buildings below the State House dome were built in the 1770's as the "Factors' Row" to house the countinghouses of agents or "factors" of mercantile firms engaged in business here. After a disastrous fire in 1883, the surviving walls were incorporated into the present structures but given a different facade.

John Shaw House, *21 State Circle.* Just beyond the statue of General DeKalb is the Shaw House which was built about 1722. This two-story frame house with a gambrel roof had a series of occupants, including a sailor and a shipwright, until 1784 when it was acquired by John Shaw, the cabinetmaker. Born in Glasgow about 1745, Shaw left Scotland for Annapolis at least as early as 1763 and worked here until his death in 1829. He provided and repaired furniture for the State House, served in the Revolution, was a vestryman of St. Anne's Parish, and also was keeper of the town's fire engine.

John Brice II House, *195 Prince George Street.* The first mayor of Annapolis, Amos Garrett, who died in 1728 and whose gravestone is in St. Anne's Churchyard, owned this property and possibly built the present house. In 1737 a prominent merchant, John Brice II, bought the house and it remained in his family until 1841. Its unusual feature is that it is set back from the street. Most small houses were built close to the street to allow more space for a garden behind it.

John Brice III House, *211 Prince George Street.* This three-story brick house, now painted grey and entered by a gracefully curving flight of iron steps, was built about 1766 by John Brice III and remodeled a century later.

Ogle Hall, *College Avenue and King George Street.* This formal Georgian House was completed in 1739 by Dr. William Stephenson who died that year. Later it was rented by Governor Samuel Ogle. Eventually it was owned by his son, Benjamin Ogle, who become governor in 1798. Benjamin enlarged the house in 1775 by adding the ballroom wing at the rear of the house. George Washington dined here in 1775, and Lafayette is said to have planted a yew tree in the garden in 1824. The house is now the headquarters of the U.S. Naval Academy Alumni Society.

U.S. Post Office. This handsome building in late Georgian style was erected in 1910 as the Post Office. In the right foreground is the Southgate Cross and fountain erected in 1901 by the citizens of the town in memory of William Southgate, who had been rector of St. Anne's from 1869 to 1899. He endeared himself to the inhabitants of the city by his attractive personality, his concern for all people, and his fondness for animals: horses, dogs, cats, and birds—indeed, as one who remembered him said, for "all things made by God in nature."

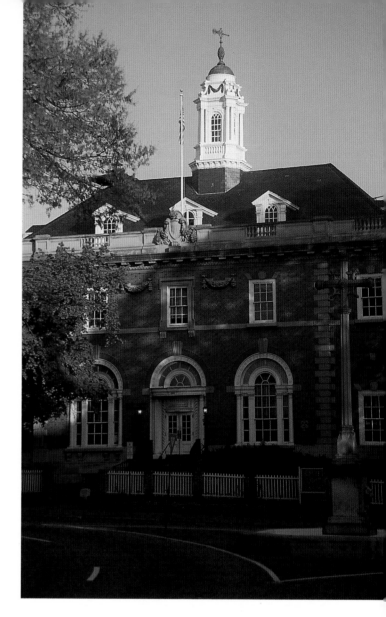

Old St. Anne's Rectory, 215-217 Hanover Street. Despite its Victorian appearance, this all-header bond house dates from the early 1760's and was the rectory of the parish until 1885. Originally it had a gable roof with end chimneys. During the occupancy of Jonathan Boucher, who was Rector of St. Anne's 1770-1772, George Washington was an occasional visitor, as his stepson, Jackie Custis, was a pupil in the school that Boucher kept here for the sons of the gentry, and Boucher put Washington up when he visited Annapolis for the races, the balls, and the theatre.

Christopher Hohne House, *45 Fleet Street.* The gray wooden house on the left was built about 1720 by Francis Holland. This gambrel-roofed, frame house with chimneys of Flemish bond is a precious survival of the kind of residence that was common in early Annapolis. It takes its name from a later occupant, Christopher Hohne, who fought in both the Revolution and the War of 1812, and who was once awarded fifty dollars by the General Assembly for helping to put out a fire that threatened the State House dome.

Overleaf
Annapolis from Spa Creek.
Approaching the City from the south, one must cross Spa Creek, in the foreground. The Naval Academy is on the right, and the State House just right of center.
Aerial photograph by Andy and Boots Michalak

Lower Main Street. The handsome late eighteenth-century house in the center was built about 1792 by Frederick Grammar, a German who had supplied bread to the armed forces during the Revolution. When it was slated for demolition in 1957, a group of concerned people incorporated under the name Port of Annapolis, Inc., bought and restored it.

Governor Calvert House, *State Circle.* Like the Bordley-Randall House, this one began in the 1720's as a smaller one. It housed Charles Calvert who was governor 1720-1727 and possibly the Lord Proprietor of Maryland, Charles, fifth Lord Baltimore, who spent the years 1731-1733 in Annapolis. But as time went on it was enlarged and remodeled, reaching its present size in Victorian days. It is now one of the city's celebrated historic inns.

Sands House, *130 Prince George Street.* Although much altered through three centuries, this small frame house with a gambrel roof and a massive central chimney is believed to be the oldest house in Annapolis and to have been built before 1700. Evan Jones kept a tavern here and was an early alderman of the city. He also served as deputy collector of customs and as assistant clerk of the Assembly. Later it was occupied successively by a joiner, a merchant, and a shipwright. About the time of the Revolution, it was bought by John Sands, a mariner and sailmaker, and it has belonged to his descendants ever since.

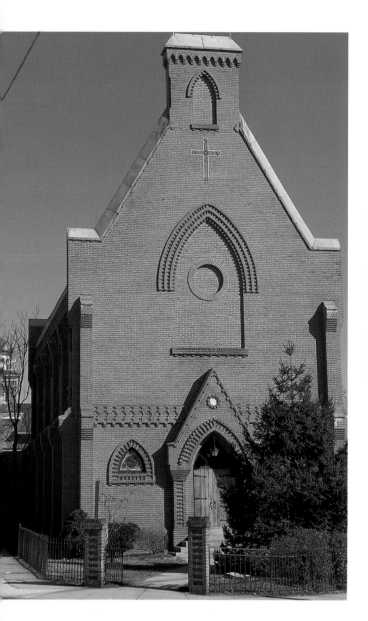

Old St. Anne's Chapel, *Prince George at East Street.* Built as a "chapel of ease" of St. Anne's Church about 1880, this Victorian Gothic brick structure was a Jewish synagogue, 1918-1962, and now houses the Chesapeake Bay Foundation which spearheads efforts to rescue the Bay from pollution and restore its pristine purity and fecundity. The picturesque building just beyond it was the Waterwitch Fire Station until recently when it was acquired by the Chesapeake Bay Foundation for additional office space. Its unusual Tuscan style and its turret and red roof have endeared it to generations of Annapolitans.

Main Street. Numbers 230–236 consist of a brick house built about 1835 by Henry Price, a "free person of color," and a frame building that may have belonged to Archibald Chisholm, the partner of the cabinetmaker John Shaw. Number 211, shown here, was built about 1820 to be the town hall of Annapolis and to house its fire engine, and continued to serve in that capacity until 1870. Number 176 was built between 1834 and 1842 by a free black named Charles Shorter.

Maryland Avenue. Radiating northeastwardly from State Circle, Maryland Avenue's fine shops are a mecca for tourists. This view is from the State House grounds just as the azaleas bloomed.

Main Street at Dusk. Known as Church Street until the turn of the century, Main Street leads from the Dock to St. Anne's Church, the steeple of which is seen silhouetted against the evening sky. The Town Clock is illuminated at night to keep passers-by apprised of the time.

Conduit Street. A row of comfortable, turn-of-the century houses
on Conduit Street near the intersection with Cathedral Street.